And we, who with unveiled faces all reflect the Lord's glory,
are being transformed into his likeness with every increasing
glory, which comes from the Lord, who is the Spirit.

2 Corinthians 3:18

To: _____

From: _____

_____

_____

_____

_____

_____

_____

_____

_____

_____

_____

_____

_____

_____

_____

_____

_____

_____

I believe God is in the business of setting us free,
making each of us into the woman he always wanted
us to be. The woman we always wanted to be.

*I am not a failure as a human being or as a
woman. In some core place deep within,
I know this. I fail, yes. But I am not a failure.
I disappoint. But I am not a disappointment.*

You are loved. Deeply. Profoundly.
Unimaginably loved.

God does not then toss us aside. He restores us—
the real us. As he heals our inner life,
he calls us to rise to the occasion of our lives.

_____

_____

_____

_____

_____

_____

_____

_____

_____

_____

_____

_____

_____

_____

_____

_____

_____

It is a beautiful paradox that the more God's
we become, the more ourselves *we become—*
the "self" he had in mind when he thought
of you before the creation of the world.

_____

_____

_____

_____

_____

_____

_____

_____

_____

_____

_____

_____

_____

_____

_____

_____

_____

_____

_____

We cannot heal ourselves or free ourselves or
save ourselves. We cannot become ourselves all
by ourselves. But we are not by ourselves.

_____

_____

_____

_____

_____

_____

_____

_____

_____

_____

_____

_____

_____

_____

_____

_____

_____

_____

_____

_____

*The temptation is to look back with regret rather
than with mercy. But God's eyes see clearly, and
they are filled with mercy. We can be merciful too.*

_____

_____

_____

_____

_____

_____

_____

_____

_____

_____

_____

_____

_____

_____

_____

_____

_____

_____

_____

*Every woman's personal struggle rooted in
her past makes her desperate for God. We all
have something that brings us to our knees.*

_____

_____

_____

_____

_____

_____

_____

_____

_____

_____

_____

_____

_____

_____

_____

_____

_____

_____

_____

_____

Forgiveness is crucial if we are to look back
in mercy at our stories. Forgiveness, like
repentance, is essential and always our choice.

_____

_____

_____

_____

_____

_____

_____

_____

_____

_____

_____

_____

_____

_____

_____

_____

Let God begin to rewrite your story.
Invite him to show you your
past through his eyes.

_____

_____

_____

_____

_____

_____

_____

_____

_____

_____

_____

_____

_____

_____

_____

_____

*Though our past has shaped us, we are not our
past. Though our failures and sin have had
an effect on who we are, we are not defined by
our failures or our sin. Jesus is our victory.*

God is coming. He has not abandoned us,
and he never will.

_The incredible capacity given to women
to bring forth life carries with it a
staggering honor and a high price._

_____

_____

_____

_____

_____

_____

_____

_____

_____

_____

_____

_____

_____

_____

_____

_____

_____

_____

*Do not curse yourself by cursing
your body or your femininity. To be
a woman is a glorious thing.*

_____

_____

_____

_____

_____

_____

_____

_____

_____

_____

_____

_____

_____

_____

_____

_____

_____

The kingdom of God will not advance
as it needs to advance without women
rising up and playing their role.

Women are image bearers of God.
Women are coheirs with Christ.
Women are valued, worthy, powerful, and needed.

We all have a deep soul hunger, and
the only satisfaction we will find for
that is in the presence of God.

_____

_____

_____

_____

_____

_____

_____

_____

_____

_____

_____

_____

_____

God restores us to the truth of who we are and the reality of the life we are living and meant to live. We are loved, wanted, seen, delighted in, provided for, cherished, chosen, known, and planned on.

_____

_____

_____

_____

_____

_____

_____

_____

_____

_____

_____

_____

_____

_____

_____

_____

_____

_____

_____

_____

God wants you to love and enjoy everything
about yourself right now and embrace
the truth that you are a beautiful woman
regardless of your measurements.

_____

_____

_____

_____

_____

_____

_____

_____

_____

_____

_____

_____

_____

_____

_____

_____

*The only reflection that really matters is
the reflection we see in God's loving and
joyous eyes. What does he see? What does
he say? He says we are beautiful now.*

_Our hope doesn't rest on our finally getting it
together. Our hope rests in Jesus. Jesus in us._

_God dreams big. And he invites us to dream
big with him. God has planted dreams
and desires in each one of our hearts._

_Being beautiful is a quality of spirit recognized
primarily in a woman whose soul is at rest because
she believes her God when he calls her lovely._

_____

_____

_____

_____

_____

_____

_____

_____

_____

_____

_____

_____

_____

_____

_____

_____

We have to choose life. Choose risk. Choose love.
The only safe place for our hearts is to dive
deeply into the magnificent, eternal, ridiculous,
overwhelming love that God has for us.

_____

_____

_____

_____

_____

_____

_____

_____

_____

_____

_____

_____

_____

_____

_____

_____

_____

_____

_____

_____

No longer bound by fear, how high can we soar?
How deep can we dive?
How much delight can we experience?

_____

_____

_____

_____

_____

_____

_____

_____

_____

_____

_____

_____

_____

_____

_____

*When we actively, by faith, lay down our fears
at the feet of Jesus, we pick up his love in return.
It is an uneven trade, a heavenly exchange.*

_____

_____

_____

_____

_____

_____

_____

_____

_____

_____

_____

_____

_____

_____

_____

_____

_____

_____

_____

_____

*The places where we still fear are simply the places
we have yet to fully receive God's love. Only by
his grace and in his love can we let our fear go.*

_A woman is a wondrous creature with a
capacity to affect her world beyond measure._

_____

_____

_____

_____

_____

_____

_____

_____

_____

_____

_____

_____

_____

_____

_____

_____

_____

_____

_____

Get a group of women together, moving toward the
same goal, and power is released. Nations are forged.
Justice is spread. The kingdom of God advances.

_____

_____

_____

_____

_____

_____

_____

_____

_____

_____

_____

_____

_____

_____

_____

_____

*Friendship is supposed to offer a taste of
what is coming when our souls will be
fully known and completely at rest.*

_____

_____

_____

_____

_____

_____

_____

_____

_____

_____

_____

_____

_____

_____

_____

_____

_____

We are meant to grow and change and
become throughout the duration of our lives,
and we need to be surrounded by people who
celebrate the person we are becoming.

_____

_____

_____

_____

_____

_____

_____

_____

_____

_____

_____

_____

_____

_____

_____

_____

_____

_____

_____

There isn't anything on earth like
relationships to make you holy.

*Let suffering be the door you walk through
that draws you to deeper intimacy with Jesus.*

Jesus understands heartbreak, betrayal,
abandonment, loneliness, sorrow, and pain.
He is acquainted with grief. He cares for you.

_____

_____

_____

_____

_____

_____

_____

_____

_____

_____

_____

_____

_____

_____

_____

_____

_____

*How do you find peace in the midst of
difficult, painful circumstances? Let Peace
find you. He's right where you are, right
smack dab in the middle of your life.*

_____

_____

_____

_____

_____

_____

_____

_____

_____

_____

_____

_____

_____

_____

_____

_____

_____

*Jesus is the only one who will never disappoint you,
never ever leave you, comfort you intimately, and
love you perfectly every single moment of your life.*

_____

_____

_____

_____

_____

_____

_____

_____

_____

_____

_____

_____

_____

_____

_____

_____

God is etching a masterpiece of stunning design.
The beauty being forged in us through the
transforming work of suffering is one that will
leave us breathless, stunned, and forever thankful.

God calls us to rise up, shake the
dust off, sit enthroned. We have a
part to play in our freedom.

_____

_____

_____

_____

_____

_____

_____

_____

_____

_____

_____

_____

_____

_____

_____

_____

_____

_____

_____

You pay too high a price to stay in chains. Freedom
is what you are made for; freedom is good.

God has given each of us an inheritance
in Christ. Jesus came that we might
have life and life to the full.

_____

_____

_____

_____

_____

_____

_____

_____

_____

_____

_____

_____

_____

_____

_____

_____

*Your inheritance in Christ is freedom and
life and joy and every good gift.
Your inheritance is victory and a heart that is
not striving or filled with fear but at rest.*

We can be so free. It all begins here—with an internal choice to let Christ so invade our hearts that we cannot be held to any sort of bondage internally.

We are no longer captives to sin. We are
no longer slaves to the Enemy, to the world,
or to our own flesh. We have been released.

_Because we belong to God, we can rest in
knowing his promises to us are true and he
is faithful. It's not a question of if God is
going to show up but how and when._

Believing God is good in the midst of
waiting is incredibly hard. Those are the
times that our faith, the treasure of our
hearts, is tested by fire and becomes gold.

Our worship of Jesus pushes back
the kingdom of darkness and
ushers in the kingdom of God.

_____

_____

_____

_____

_____

_____

_____

_____

_____

_____

_____

_____

_____

_____

_____

_____

_____

Let us then remember who we truly are.
Let us go further up and further in to all
the riches and the joy and the intimacy
and the healing that God has for us!

Jesus beckons us onward. He beckons us upward. Let's press on to the goal that is set before us—to become fully transformed, fully alive, fully ourselves, fully his.

BECOMING MYSELF JOURNAL
Published by David C Cook
4050 Lee Vance View
Colorado Springs, CO 80918 U.S.A.

David C Cook Distribution Canada
55 Woodslee Avenue, Paris, Ontario, Canada N3L 3E5

David C Cook U.K., Kingsway Communications
Eastbourne, East Sussex BN23 6NT, England

The graphic circle C logo is a registered trademark of David C Cook.

ISBN 978-0-7814-1214-8

© 2014 Stasi Eldredge
Published in association with Yates & Yates, www.yates2.com.

Quotes taken from Becoming Myself © 2013 Stasi Eldredge,
ISBN 978-1-4347-0535-8

Printed in the United States of America
First Edition 2014

1 2 3 4 5 6 7 8 9 10

013114